Charles Henry Pullen

Miss Columbia's public school, or, Will it blow over?

Charles Henry Pullen

Miss Columbia's public school, or, Will it blow over?

ISBN/EAN: 9783741170744

Manufactured in Europe, USA, Canada, Australia, Japa

Cover: Foto ©Thomas Meinert / pixelio.de

Manufactured and distributed by brebook publishing software
(www.brebook.com)

Charles Henry Pullen

Miss Columbia's public school, or, Will it blow over?

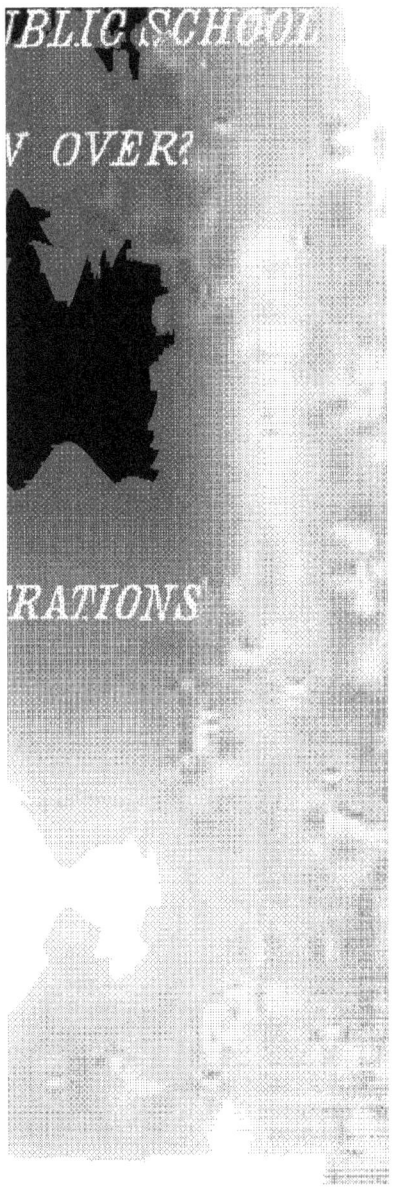

UBLIC SCHOOL

V OVER?

RATIONS

MISS COLUMBIA'S
PUBLIC SCHOOL;

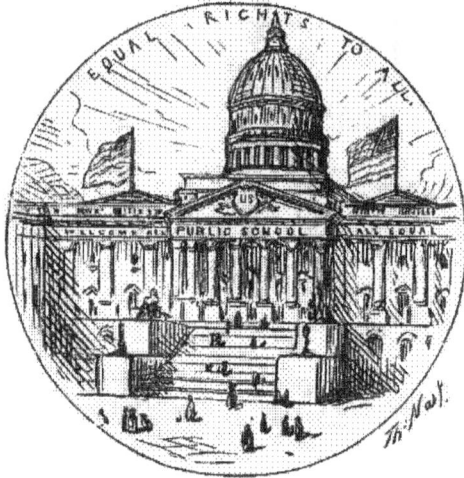

or,

WILL IT BLOW OVER?

BY A. COSMOPOLITAN.

WITH 72 ILLUSTRATIONS BY

THOMAS NAST.

' It is only a matter of time."—FATHER HECKER.

"'The American idea must give way, and with it whatever contradicts or does not accord with the Catholic idea."—THE TABLET.

New York:

FRANCIS B. FELT & CO.

1871.

THEIR AIM.

MISS COLUMBIA'S SCHOOL.

MISS COLUMBIA kept a large public school, which included every possible description of boy. All colors were represented, all nationalities, all classes, and all sects.

It was, as may be imagined, a somewhat difficult task to preserve harmony among so many scholars of different characteristics, but as long as there was fair play all round, and partiality shown to none, Miss Columbia managed to sustain her own institution firmly in its original principles.

The foundation of our Republic.

The original plan of the school was to allow all the scholars the most perfect freedom, and to submit to them for approval the rules by which they should be managed; thus making their government the will of the scholars.

As long as the majority of the boys were patriotic, orderly, honest, and had the interest and honor of the school at heart, this plan would work well; but as soon as corruption, treachery, dishonesty, and partiality crept in, a school conducted upon such principles would be shaken to its very foundations, and, perhaps, ultimately ruined.

There had been many little tiffs in this school, as in every other, but none of a serious character, until

EQUAL RIGHTS TO ALL.
NO ESTABLISHED CHURCH
RELIGIOUS LIBERTY
FREEDOM OF SPEECH
OR OF THE PRESS
FREEDOM OF CARICATURING
THE RIGHT OF THE PEOPLE PEACEABLY
TO ASSEMBLE AND TO PETITION FOR
A REDRESS OF GRIEVANCES.

THE FIRST LESSONS.

a great "unpleasantness" arose between a Northern and a Southern boy, about a little colored boy, whom the Southern boy claimed as his property—a claim entirely inconsistent with the fundamental principle on which the school was based, viz., that all the scholars were born free and equal.

This disagreement about the colored boy had been a threatening cloud from the time the school was first organized; but it was thought that, if left to time, it would pass away of itself.

"Take him, if you dare."

Instead of that, however, it grew and grew, and at length assumed such vast proportions that a line had to be drawn across the grounds, where the claims of

†the Southern boy could, or could not, be recognized. 'The disputes growing out of this distinction so em-bittered the feelings of the Northern and Southern boys against each other, that at last their smoldering

Terrible blows.

passions broke out into terrible blows—such blows that Miss Columbia herself was astonished at their strength; and all Dame Europa's school lifted up

Our neutral friends.

their hands in virtuous horror, and exclaimed, "Can such things be?"

Our little cousin, Johnny Bull, was especially pleased at the big fight, and kept saying to all the boys in Dame Europa's school, "Didn't I told you so?"

He jumped for joy when the fight began, and would have turned a regular somersault, had he not bethought himself that his island was small, and he might roll over into the water.

Neutral John.

He saw a good opportunity for lengthening out the fight, and turning a penny at the same time, by supplying the little Southern boy with implements of warfare.

The invasion of Mexico.

Then there was little Johnny Crapeau, too, who thought he, also, might take advantage of the scrimmage to help himself to some of Miss Columbia's grounds, and extend the sway of the "Latin race." So, in order to be ready at the right moment, he imported some French frogs into Mexican territory, just south of the school. But that ruse proved a failure; most of the frogs died, or were squelched out; their leader was shot, and the rest were forced to return to Johnny Crapeau all the worse for the wear.

Meantime the fighting continued so fiercely in Miss Columbia's school as to sometimes endanger the life of Miss Columbia herself; but the loyal Northern boys always proved strong enough to protect her person.

The combat was protracted and bloody, and there was no lack of courage on either side; but, finally, at the end of the fourth round, the Southern boy

"Shake hands."

threw up the sponge; and the result was that the colored boy had rights which the white boy was bound to respect.

But Miss Columbia's duties now became more complicated than ever; for the bitter feeling engendered by the late contest frequently exhibited itself, and was hard to control, as is always the case in every school after a rumpus.

There were here, as elsewhere, plenty of mean-spirited little boys who, for malicious purposes of their own, did their best to keep up the remembrance of the fight and renew the disturbance.

It seemed best to Miss Columbia, as a punishment to the Southern boy for his past misconduct, to put him on his good behavior for the time being, by depriving him of any voice whatever in school matters— a privilege which she now bestowed upon the colored boy. This plan she thought would have a salutary effect upon the Southern boy, and bring him to a realizing sense of his past injustice; but, on the contrary, it seemed to irritate him all the more. To behold his former chattel elevated to authority over him was more than his haughty spirit could tolerate. It also made him very sulky to see a portion of the Northern boys, who had lately been fighting him, come and plant themselves upon his own section, and try to manipulate the colored boy with a single eye to their own interests.

This unsettled state of things troubled Miss Columbia exceedingly, and she began to feel that it was time to adopt a different course, as matters kept growing worse instead of better. She thought that restoring the Southern boy to his former power in the school might have the desired effect, and bring about the much-needed reconciliation. She was all the more desirous of effecting a perfect union, in order to gain strength against a common enemy, whose underhand inffluence, she had begun to discover, was undermining her great public school.

So one day, when the boys were all assembled, she propounded her views to them, and waited to hear theirs.

Miss Columbia's appeal.

"Now, dear boys," she began, "I want the earnest

attention of all of you. The constant disagreements among you have for some time past occasioned me great pain and anxiety; and I feel sure that, if such a state of things continues, the prosperity and progress of the school will be seriously retarded. Now, what do you say to giving our little Southerner his former voice in all school matters? Let us bury the hatchet forever, and let by-gones be by-gones. His fault was a very serious one, and he has received a severe punishment; but we are protected from any repetition of his past folly by the Fourteenth and Fifteenth Amendments of our rules, which have been written down in letters of blood, and can never be wiped out; and woe be to him who ever makes the rash attempt!"

Discordant sounds greeted these remarks; and it was evident that they were not received with unanimous approval by the boys.

The head boy, who, during the fray, had been in the very thickest of it, seemed the most willing to adopt Miss Columbia's proposition; but, seeing the evident dissatisfaction around him, and having no more voice than any of the other boys in the school rules, he remained passive in his seat, although the words, "Let us have peace," seemed to escape his lips involuntarily.

It was noticed that the boys who had kept their own skins the soundest, and were farthest from the

" Let us have peace."

place where the blows were struck, were loudest in
their objections—particularly some who had gained for
themselves a reputation as reformers. They had kept
themselves prominently before the school for years, and
were among the first to agitate the doctrine of equal
rights to all colors; and as long as the cause for it
existed, no mortal could deny their sincerity or their
ability as its champions.

But that fatal love of notoriety which seems to get
the best of all our prominent small boys, and is,
perhaps, a limit set by Providence to human importance, in due time overtook our reformers. Since the
colored boy had been granted his just rights, they

THE CHAIRMAN OF THE HANGING COMMITTEE.

tried to stir up other agitations, such as the doctrine of baby-suffrage, etc. But as boys are always awkward in handling babies, they never seemed to get the hang of their new hobby, and it didn't "take" among the school as the old one did; therefore, they were only too ready, when the least occasion presented itself, to go back to the old hobby, at which they had won their early laurels.

Finally, the general dissatisfaction found voice, and a Northern boy rose and said, "But look here, Miss Columbia, that is all very nice about joining hands, and forgetting the past; but how about these sneaking little skunks that call themselves the K. K. K.'s, who pommel our boys, both white and colored, whenever they get a chance? We can't submit to that, and they don't deserve that we should; no, ma'am!"

And a chorus of voices broke in here, saying,

"No; they deserve hanging better!"

One voice, louder than the rest, was heard to say,

"Yes, yes, let's be afther hanging the *nagur*, by all manes."

This voice emanated from a boy who had been uncommonly active during a certain July scrimmage, still fresh in the recollection of the whole school.

He was the most turbulent and unruly boy in the school, and never understood any subject intelligently; but whenever personal violence was threatened, he was *there*.

The uproar culminated here, and Miss Columbia called out, " Silence !" several times before order was restored. It took her longer than most school-mistresses to enforce her commands, as each boy was impressed with a deep sense of his own importance and responsibility in the affairs of government, and each considered himself supreme ruler.

Calling the school to order.

" Tut, tut, for shame !" she said ; "just consider what an expense you would be at for rope, if you were to try and hang all the corrupt law-breakers and treacherous law-makers among you Northern boys ! But hanging is not to the point ; the rope's end will not be the end of our troubles, and you cannot be too dainty ; for we see plenty of outrages among the Tammany tribe of Indians over there, but who ever hears of hanging the wrong-doers ?

" ' Let us have peace ! ' as our head boy says, and let us show malice to none and charity to all. It is true that

K. K. K.'s exist, in defiance of all the rules of the school, but my hope is that, with a better mutual understanding, these things will die out of their own accord. Our Southern boy will soon see that the course he is now pursuing injures himself more than anybody else, and deters many a well-meaning and energetic Northern boy from settling as his neighbor, and making his naturally attractive side of the school-grounds the most charming place in the world. Some of the boys who already represent you there are not angels by any means, and have aggravated the Southerner's sense of wrong by trying to get the best of him, and squeezing more almighty dollars out of him than they can out of the rest of you, since you are a match for each other on your own grounds—that fondly worshiped dollar before which you all bow."

Put that in your pipe and smoke it.

The boys did not quite relish these remarks. If Miss Co
lumbia had taken handfuls of their golden idol, and thrown
it at them and hit them in the face ever so hard, they would
have scrambled for it eagerly. But to be thus insulted
gratuitously with the shadow and not the substance made
them wince uneasily. Miss Columbia here resumed: "You
have all got to live together; so let these constant bickerings
cease. I love our little Southern scholar just as dearly as I do
any of the rest of you, and have his interests and his advancement just as much at heart, and I long to see harmony restored between you brothers, for he *is* your own brother,
though he has sinned in the past. How does a wise mother
act toward an erring son? After administering what
she considers a proper punishment, does she keep on prob-

"Bind up his wounds."

ing his wounds by constant reminders of his past faults?
No! justice once rendered, she makes haste to heal
the scar by all the soothing arts she knows of, and
finds the lesson none the less salutary on that account.
Now boys will be boys, whether in school or at home,
and why will not the same principles work here, if you only
try to carry them out?   You were the victors; therefore it
becomes you to be magnanimous, and so let us bury the hatchet.

"Other boys, too, feel that it is well to hold out the olive-branch sometimes; for instance, see your cousin Johnny Bull, who has taken the initiative, and come all the way across the water to settle the dispute between you, in the most manly and straightforward manner — an act

The High Joints

Commission.

which redounds to his infinite credit and honor. He does

not feel that his dignity is compromised in the smallest degree, nor would yours be by making similar overtures.

"Then, too, my dear boys, I fear that in hardening yourselves toward your Southern brother, and teaching yourselves to ignore his fraternal claims upon you, your own characters have sadly deteriorated, your moral senses are becoming blunted, your integrity, your honor and pride in the school have given way before a selfish and eager desire for the rapid advancement of individual interests. Heretofore it has always been a credit to a boy to say that he was brought up in my school; but if these injurious habits continue to gain upon you, it will soon be a disgrace. Each boy must feel that all must sacrifice something for the sake of the general good.

"I want to recall to your memory that fable of Æsop's, familiar to you all, where a man carries two bags, one before him and one behind him. The one in front of him is marked, 'Other people's faults,' and the one behind him is 'his own' faults. Of course the one in front of him is constantly before his eyes, but he never sees the one behind.

"Apply this to your case. Just mark the bag in front of you 'South,' and the one behind you 'North,' and I want you to take the time to examine more carefully the one behind you than you have been in the habit of doing. It is now time for recess. Go, then, and think the matter over at your leisure, and as soon as you feel that you have made some discoveries, and found out some of your own sins, come to me for further advice."

The bell then rang and school adjourned, the boys separating, and each following his own inclination. Some, giving no heed to Miss Columbia's words, went to play, and thought no more of the subject under discussion; others went straight to their workshops, as they never lost a minute or an opportunity of coining dollars, while a few took their teacher's injunction to heart, and did really try to ponder out the problem before them.

That night the Northern boy did not sleep as tranquilly as usual, and when at length he fell into a troubled doze, after tossing about uneasily for hours, he was visited by dreams of evil omen.

Look out for the Locomotive!

He dreamed of St. Peter's at Rome, which, he thought,
instead of being a sacred edifice, was merely a large political machine in the form of a locomotive, and had as head
engineer an old man wearing a huge helmet-shaped hat,
on which was inscribed, "The infallible one." He had
always thought that institution belonged to Dame Europa's
school, but there he saw that many of the tracks had been

Disuniting Church and State.

torn up, and the huge machine did not run smoothly any
more ; and what was his horror and consternation at seeing
these replaced by many new tracks, just put down, which
ran right through Miss Columbia's grounds and intersected
them in every direction·! Some of these tracks he remem-

bered having seen before, but what now astonished him
was the immense increase in their number, the firm and
secure manner in which they were riveted to the earth, and
the enormous extent of ground they covered.   There were
miles and miles of them; in fact, the country was grid-
ironed with them.

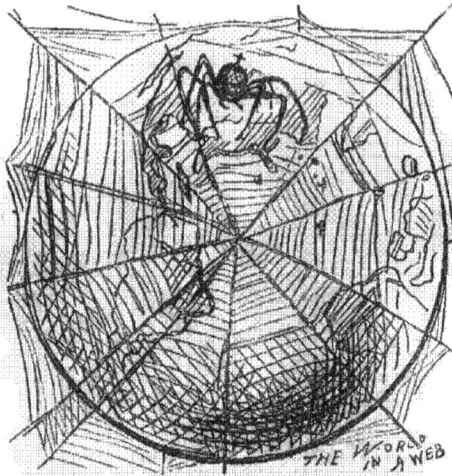

THE WORLD IN A WEB

He wondered how the right to possess the ground had
ever been placed in the power of the vast machine.   He
saw, employed upon the tracks, Pat, the Irish boy, who always did that kind of work, but he now perceived that his
overseer appeared to be a Jesuit whom he had often noticed
prowling around the school of late, and he appeared to
draw his grants of land and his supplies of money from

THE CAT'S-PAW.

a certain office which had a "Big Six" on the door, and was situated in the largest and most important depot.

He recognized among the most prominent officials in this depot the faces of many boys which were familiar to him every day in school. The Jesuit seemed to be holding out to them, in return for the money and the land, the promise of the Irish boy's influence and voice in the school, that it should always be in favor of these corrupt officials, and that he would do his best to retain them in authority continually. They had a large portion of the school under their influence already, but nothing less than the whole of it would satisfy their ambition. Then he dreamt that the infallible engineer took entire charge of the school, and established

In Miss Columbia's chair.

himself in Miss Columbia's chair. Turning in loathing from such rule, he tries to find the Bible bequeathed to him by his Puritan father, and search in its pages for comfort; but lo! the form of the infallible one seems to envelop it with a pall of darkness; he cannot see the page

Burning the Bible.

before him; in vain he struggles to retain his grasp of it, but it has been wrenched from him; it is gone!

At this, he awoke and gave a sigh of relief as he thought to himself that it was only a nightmare vision.

But the dream continued to haunt him, and it was with a kind of terror and misgiving that he repaired to his seat in the school-room at the usual time.

" 'Twas but a dream."

In opening the school Miss Columbia took up the Bible, to read some selections, according to her invariable custom, but as she turned its pages, a dark frown was visible on her face, which, somehow, struck a chill to the heart of our dreamer. She read on, however, without interruption ; but when she had finished, she turned toward the boys, as she closed the book, and said:

"Some one has been tampering with my Bible again, and left his dirty finger-marks upon it. This thing has happened before, but I refrained from saying anything about it, and now I don't want it to happen again, or I shall speak plainer. I know well enough which of you boys it

TAMPERING WITH THE BIBLE.

is, and I fear that I have been too lenient and indulgent to
him hitherto, and that he thinks to take the very meanest
advantage of it, and is about to repay me with the basest
ingratitude. There are some of the privileges properly
belonging to you other boys, of which I have been obliged
to deprive you, simply because this troublesome boy
abused his liberties. But if none of you large boys,
whose business it is to right such things, will leave your
selfish pursuits for a short time to bring him to a sense of
his duties, I myself will take him in hand and give him
such a thrashing as will not only astonish this school, but
all the other schools in the universe," and Miss Columbia's
eyes flashed in a manner that showed that she meant to be
as good as her word. The work of the school then went
on as usual, but at recess our dreamer sought out Miss
Columbia, who was thoughtfully pacing up and down the
empty school-room, and told her his vision of the preced-
ing night, and that, when she made the remarks about the

Flight of the Jesuit.

Bible, it seemed to confirm it, and made him fear that it was prophetic.

Miss Columbia listened to him in silence, and when he had told her all, she said :

"Come, my boy, let us walk around the play-ground quietly. I have something to show you "—and they passed out by a side door, so as not to attract the attention of the other boys, or disturb their play—when Miss Columbia suddenly exclaimed, "Ah, yes, there he is again. See him !"

The Foundation.

as a black figure darted out slyly from among the boys, crept
stealthily round through an alley-way and disappeared.

Our dreamer, looking in the direction indicated by her
gaze, recognized the form of the Jesuit of his dream.

It seemed to give Miss Columbia no surprise, as she had
often come upon him in the same manner before. They
walked on until they came near the spot which the Jesuit
had just left, when Miss Columbia, examining the foundation of the building, said with a sigh, " Yes, yes ; I see he
has been at it again—and this is the thing that I wish to
call your attention to. Do you see that some of the foundation stones have been removed, and carried off; only a
little at a time has disappeared, not enough to excite re-
mark, but still by degrees enough has been taken away to
leave a wide gap, and if this thing is allowed to continue,
enough will soon be gone to make the building shaky and
insecure, and the whole edifice will eventually be under-
mined. One of the largest pieces was carried off quite
recently, but it was done in such a bold and defiant manner
that it drew the attention of some of the larger boys, who,
without saying anything to me, got some planks and
beams from the platform erected for the meeting lately
held to indorse the Union of the Italian school, which may
fill up the gap temporarily. But we cannot go on bolster-
ing up our school in this way. If we allow much more of
the foundation to be abstracted, the school *must* stop."

Our boy stood aghast; he had not dared to own to himself before that this evil influence had become so active. He had often been made to feel its power, but he had tried to disguise the truth and deceive himself, by calling the evil by another name.

Miss Columbia watches him closely, and tries to discover what effect this revelation has upon him, but he gives no outward sign as yet, and she says,

"Come, let us return to the school-room. I have something else to show you there," and they retrace their steps.

Just as they are about to re-enter the school-room, they both perceive the sly little Irish boy in the very act of seizing the Bible and throwing it out of the window. At

"Put that Bible back!"

the sight of this dastardly deed, the little spark of patriotism left in our Northern boy flames up; he forgets his
money-making and his all-engrossing private affairs for a
few minutes; his cold exterior melts away; he loses his
marvelous powers of self-control; he rushes at the Irish
boy, seizes him by the throat and cries out imperiously,
"Put that Bible back!"

The Irish boy cowers beneath the flashing eyes of his
school-fellow, replaces the book, and steals away, muttering
to himself, "I'll be even with you yet. My time is soon
coming."

Miss Columbia nods approvingly at her companion, and
says, "Well done; I may have hopes of you yet." "Now,"
she continues, "I want you to come here and look at these
books, and see how they also have been tampered with.
You remember the nice arithmetic we used to have; that
has been removed, and one put in its place by Slippery
Dick, and you know well enough how *he* keeps accounts.
We now have Book-keeping by Jim, Jr., and Erie Gould,
Geography and Surveying by the Boss, Widening and
Straightening by his partner Peter Bee, Practical Educa-
tion by a man whose Sands of life have nearly run out,
Grammar by Teddy O'Flannigan (New York Alderman),
Gymnastics by Pokey Hall, Theology by Father O'Bigotry,
and so on through the whole list of studies.

"Now, you know books like these are not the kind of
material with which to educate the rising generation of this

A CHANGE OF TEXT-BOOKS.

school. You could not even maintain the standard of in-
telligence at its present point, to say nothing of advancing
as you should. You cannot but already feel the baleful
influence of the powerful cliques and " rings " which have
been formed of late within the school ; they levy the most
unmerciful tolls upon you for every conceivable pretext,
and you know that they exert a most deadening influence
on many of your enterprising pursuits ; they have become so
arrogant and exacting that, in order to be permitted to carry
on your ordinary avocations, you are obliged to truckle to
them, which is the most degrading kind of slavery, as it
confuses your standard of right and wrong, and you lose
your self-respect. You grow so accustomed to seeing
virtue punished and vice rewarded that you will soon come
to regard it as the natural and proper order of things."

The boy listened with grave attention, and when Miss
Columbia ceased speaking, he said, "Yes, I see what you
mean now. I shall speak to the other boys, and see if we
can't decide on some plan to get us out of these ugly
snarls."

Miss Columbia answered with a sigh, "You can try it ;
but now do you understand why I wished you to be rec-
onciled to your Southern brother more than ever ? Do
you not see that while you two, the original pupils of my
school, are contending with each other, those who have
only come among us lately will usurp all your rights, and,

" *You'd* better leave. There's not room for both."

in fact, it will only be the story of the camel over again, and you know such a monopoly as that would be intolerable to both of you. Have you held out your hand to him yet ?"

The boy here looked abashed, and said, " No, I have not; he has done things quite recently that fairly make my blood boil ! "

Here the boys came into school again and took their seats, and lessons went on as usual. When the school was dismissed, and while the boys were still lingering about the play-ground, our Northern boy went up to the Irish boy and said to him :

" Ain't you going to apologize to Miss Columbia for what you did to-day ? Don't you know this is her school, and that you owe it to her to do so ?"

" Apologize to a heretic is it ?" inquired the Irish boy, with a sneer.

" Why not ? It is through her that you enjoy all your privileges, and she has always been too kind to you. Were you not warmed at her hearth-stone ?"

The Ribbonman.

" Let her go to blazes. And I'll be after breaking your mug, too, some of these nights ; it's only a matter of time. And then, when I've thrashed you, I'll put a head on these same smart Yankees who are now making a tool of me because of my strength. I know what I'm about, and ain't such a big fool as they think. Sure, this is our promised land, and we're bound to have it, and if you don't like it, sure you can leave it. You haven't had any time to take care of it yourself, so I'll do it for you. The Pope himself is going to sit in Miss Columbia's chair, and she can be afther looking for another place."

The Northern boy, dismayed and disgusted, turned away, and, as he walked on, he encountered another Irish boy who wore a yellow ribbon. Knowing that there is the deepest antagonism between him and the boy he had just left, he appealed to him, and asked him if he would be on his side in case of a row with the other one. He received a sympathetic answer, but he was reminded by the boy with the yellow ribbon that he, too, had a bone to pick with him.

The Orangeman.

"You remember," said he, "one day not very long ago, when that boy over there and his comrades, set upon us like a pack of wolves, while we were harmlessly and decorously enjoying ourselves on a certain holiday of ours? You call this a school of freedom for all, and yet they slaughtered us right and left, and you never dared lift a hand or say a word against it. We ourselves paid them back in their own coin, and defended ourselves as well as we were able. Then they threatened us that we dared not march through the grounds again; they would not allow it; they would stand ready at every turn with shillalahs and firearms and kill us and stone us as we went.

"But not being made of cowardly stuff, we intended to celebrate our next holiday as usual, when *you* came whining to us not to break the peace.

"We weren't going to break the peace; we were simply going to have the same rights and privileges as the rest

of the boys, especially he, who blockades the whole school-
ground on his holiday, and woe to him who dares cross
his path. *He* may do all this with impunity and you

"Clear the streets."

never raise your voice against him.   Indeed, you are so
overawed by this gigantic bully that a day will soon come
when you will even be afraid to cross the grounds with
your own flag.   You ought to have protected me on my
holiday, and if you couldn't have done it yourself, you
should have appealed to Miss Columbia to call out the
army and navy boys to do it.   It is high time for you
to show that the rest of the boys have rights which even
the Irish Catholic boy is bound to respect in this school
of liberty and equality.   But, my boy, when the crisis
comes, and you get your eyes wide open and see things as

they are, and call them by their right names, I'm your man and there's my hand on it," and the warm-hearted Irish boy grasped him heartily by the hand.

Our boy, a little comforted, walked on to the group of Tammany boys, who were standing together laughing and talking. The spot where they stood was noticeable for its brilliancy, owing to the glitter and flash of the enormous diamonds which they all wore. Some were as big as your fist, others as big as your head, and some of the boys seemed to be completely encrusted with them. As he approached them they looked at him defiantly, and when he broached his subject to them, they received his remarks with shouts of derisive laughter, and said, "Well,

" What are you going to do about it ?

what are you going to do about it?" whereupon one of

them stepped up to him and slipped a couple of dollars into his hand, saying, " There, there, shut up and be off." But he dropped their filthy money as if he had been stung, whereat one of them cried out, " Oh, give him some more! That ain't his price."

Another boy, who was standing near by eating an orange, rushed up and seized the money and pocketed it in the boldest manner. At this the Tammany boys all chuckled triumphantly, and exclaimed:

" That's a cheap orange ; now what's *your* price ?"

He made no reply, but walked back, with a sickening sense of humiliation and defeat, as he began to realize how exultant and secure this "ring" of Tammany boys had grown to be. One thing he vowed inwardly—that none of them should ever be head boy in school, if they tried ever so hard.

Now he heard the noise of several trumpets, sounded by various boys around the grounds, and the Tammany boys seemed to be greatly discomfited and annoyed thereby. The tunes seemed obnoxious to them, and they were so loud. Their ringleader suggested throwing the trumpeters some pennies, and the others hastened to carry out this direction, which appeared to have the desired effect upon some of them instantly, as they immediately changed the tune and played very softly; but others were proof against such allurements, and continued to play the same tune just as loudly and boldly as before, and the

Tammany boys tried to resume their customary composure and effrontery in spite of them.

Our boy had not the heart to discuss his subject further, so he went sadly to his own room.

Tax.

During his absence he found that another layer of tacks had been laid on all his furniture. Everything had been crowded with tacks pretty thickly before, here and in school, and also on the grounds ; but these last were larger and more objectionable than any heretofore, which deprived him of all comfort, and made his burdens well-nigh intolerable.

He knew well enough that this last aggravation was the work of the Tammany boys, and that it was upon the proceeds of this that they depended for their big diamonds and other luxuries, including the favor and benediction of the Roman Catholic Church—a stupendously expensive luxury, but one that always insured them the good-will of the Irish boy, on whom they relied to reinstate them in power every term. And the Irish boy's strength had never failed to retain the best places for his own chosen.

The room grows dark, and our boy begins to feel a little drowsy, when his attention is aroused by a gentle tapping at his door, which he opens, and beholds the burly form of Hans, his German friend and comrade, and, moreover, one of the quietest, steadiest, and most orderly boys in school.

A friend in need, and a friend, indeed!

"Good evening, Hans; come in and sit down. I'm real glad to see you, by Jove! Your the very fellow to help us now."

As Hans came in and seated himself, our boy was aston-ished at his *physique*, and thought that he must be **more**

powerful than the Irish boy, as he seemed to have grown
so much of late.

"Well, Hans," he said, "I congratulate you upon the
splendid conquest that your head boy, William, has gained
for himself in Dame Europa's school. He has my best
wishes, and I am sure he deserves them."

The fight in Dame Europa's School.

"Yes," said Hans, "every boy in school says the same
thing to me, except that discontented, envious Irish boy,
who always cries, 'Hurrah for the French!'"

"So you dislike him, too, do you?"

"Yes, I do that," said Hans emphatically. "I can't submit to Irish rule and love him. Don't you think that I
know the power he has been gaining for himself so stealthily in Miss Columbia's school?"

"Well, then, Hans, why don't you come and help me
keep him in his place? You are always so mum
in all school matters that it is hard to tell which side
you are on. You avail yourself of all our privileges,
but keep perfect silence, and appear to take no interest in what is passing. If you had joined your voice

to mine before, this evil could never have grown so threatening."

"Ah! yes, that is all very nice, but why don't you go to *him* for help if you want any? You show him partiality in everything else. Why is it that, when any Irish boy who has been in this school goes over to Dame Europa's, and kicks up a row with Johnny Bull, and gets arrested, as he deserves, for his misconduct, there are always plenty of Miss Columbia's boys ready to get up in school and make

Unbottled.

buncombe speeches about 'the American incarcerated in Johnny Bull's Bastile.' Then, when Johnny Bull sees how dearly he is beloved here, he sends him back again, and all parties run to meet him, and receive him with

THE WELCOME TO NEW CORK.

honors, and shake his hands. It is just a big bid for his voice next term, and you know it, but you never got his support yet, and you never will.

" Why is it that when some of my brothers, who had joined the school here, went over to Dame Europa's school on a visit, and were made to join the army boys there against their will, and applied to this school for protection, there was not a single voice heard here on their behalf? I waited and waited to hear some response, but in vain."

His listener answered with a groan: " Yes, that is too true, Hans."

" Then, again," resumed Hans, " see how my privileges are curtailed—for no offense of my own, either. I come here, and conform to all the rules of the school. I bring the same social habits that I have always been allowed in Dame Europa's school, where the rules are much more strict than here. I am allowed, for awhile, to retain the same rights that I have been accustomed to at home.

Quiet enjoyment.

One of them is, after I have faithfully done my week's hard work, to sit in my garden on Sunday, smoke my pipe, sip my glass of lager, and enjoy the music. I do this in the company of my parents and my brothers and sisters. It is a harmless and innocent enough amusement, and interferes with no one.

" But the Irish boy opposite gulps down whisky by the quart, gets raving drunk, murders somebody, and then the cry is raised, Monday morning, '*The Dutch boy must give up his lager*, because the Irish boy breaks the peace on the Sabbath day.' Then your boys make another rule, and I am deprived of my liberty, because the Irish boy abuses his. Your own boys all use their voices against me, because they drink all they want during the week, and even in school hours they whisper to one another, 'Come, let's take a drink,' and then they slip out, and go to the bar-

Nipping.

room round the corner; and you know that many a boy gets so muddled over his book-keeping in the afternoon that he often sees double, and puts down noughts where they don't belong. Then he stalks solemnly to church, with a sanctimonious face, on Sunday, looking too good ever to taste a drop of liquor, or soil a floor with tobacco-juice, and passes us, contemptuously exclaiming: 'Oh!

"Oh! those infidel Dutch boys!"

those infidel Dutch boys.' The white-headed boy who makes the greatest outcry against my Sunday, the one who has the loudest trumpet, exclaims through it that we Dutch boys love our lager better than we do Miss Columbia or her school; but I believe he would rather see the whole school go to smash than let us drink lager on Sunday. If that is his allegiance to Miss Columbia, it don't amount to much. You appeal to me to side with you, but are you fair to me? Then, again, justice is a mere farce in this section. What chance has a decent boy to get his rights here? Your Tammany bench has grown so rotten and so foully decayed that a decent boy can't sit on it any more, and yet you go on grinding out your dollars, and paying no more attention to it than if it was a matter of no moment to you."

"Well, as to money-making, friend Hans, I don't see but what we row in the same boat."

Hans here winked knowingly, and replied: "Yes, that is all right—but we don't sell body and soul to an imperial ring and call it smartness. Now, how can we give you the weight of our voice in school matters unless we are assured of enjoying our national privilege? We have given you ample proof that we will not misuse it, as you must have seen already."

The Northern boy chafed somewhat impatiently under Hans' lengthy harangue, but still was glad to have heard him speak his mind so freely.

Hans now, having relieved his mind, rose to depart, when the boys shook hands heartily, and both felt that they should understand each other better in future.

Our boy flings himself upon his bed, and falls asleep, and again the contending feelings in his mind cause him uneasy dreams.

He dreams of Saint Bartholomew's massacre—that, as history repeats itself, so he was on the point of witnessing a repetition of that horrible slaughter. He thought the scene was the school, and that the actors in it were the Greeks whose faces he was so familiar with every day.

At first, all was panic, confusion, and precipitate flight, but Miss Columbia, quickly recovering her self-possession, sounded the alarm, and gave him the signal to advance. He stepped forward, and the boys all rallied around him rapidly. At his right hand was his Southern brother.

Reunited.

Their eyes met, their hands clasped in an iron grip, and the Puritan and the Huguenot forgot their mutual grievances, and were strong brothers in arms, as of old, against one common enemy.

Both seized the dear old flag, and waving it proudly aloft, each pledged himself to be forever faithful to it.

There was Hans; there was the Irish Orange boy and many liberal Catholics; there was the Jew; there were the Protestants of all nationalities; there were all the heretics and infidels, and even the heathen Chinee, on his side.

Then the Tammany boys, thinking these would probably

be victorious, wished to join them also, but the others pushed them off indignantly, and cried out, " Go fight with

" This is not your *forte*."

your own chosen scum ; we want no more traitors in our camp."

Then ensued a fearful struggle, but it was short and de-cisive. The boys fought like lions for the liberty which they were determined not to resign, and the pent-up wrath

Victory.

THE SURRENDER OF THE HESSIANS.

of years burst forth with a fury which astonished themselves. Then, when the struggle was over, and the victors
had quietly settled back to their old pursuits (with this
difference, that Puritan and Huguenot pursue their studies
seated affectionately side by side), Dame Europa sends to
congratulate Miss Columbia on having rid herself of the
danger which menaced her, and says that she has a sugges-
tion to make.

The compact.

She proposes to give up the Isle of Erin to the exclusive use of the Greeks, upon which they may establish a Republic founded on their own ideas of perfect freedom and liberty, she never having been able to satisfy their demands in that respect, and Miss Columbia's school, also, having fallen far short of their ideal.   She proposes to collect them

Universal Thanksgiving Day.

all from the four quarters of the globe, where, she has no doubt, they will be most willingly given up, and to have them all transported to the Isle of Erin; furnish them with all their demands, arms, ammunition, rum, whisky, etc.; but no vessels of any kind are to be allowed, as she wishes none to

Ireland blockaded.

leave the island, which is to be guarded by a large fleet, in order to secure to the inhabitants the uninterrupted enjoyment of peace and happiness, which will reign supreme.

This treaty was signed by Dame Europa and Miss Columbia, and carried out with scrupulous fidelity.

Ten years seemed to elapse, and everything appeared to be very quiet and peaceful on the Isle of Erin, when the signers of the treaty became exceedingly curious to ascertain the result of their experiment, and determined to visit it. They approached the coast with great caution, so as not to disturb any innocent enjoyment, but not a sound broke the stillness; it was peace itself.

Not a creature is in sight. They come nearer; they land; everything seems to be growing most luxuriantly, but where are the Greeks?

Where are the Greeks?

They then scoured the island, but could not find a soul. Dame Europa and Miss Columbia went in different directions, and finally met at the starting-point, but found not a living thing, and both exclaimed in a chorus of thanksgiv-

Peace at last.

ing, " Thank Heaven ! they have had their liberty, and now they rest in peace !"

He awoke feeling as if a great weight had been lifted from him, but after all it was only a dream, and he had the full measure of his difficulties still to contend against.

Pleasant dreams.

After school was over that day, our Northern boy encountered the Orange boy on the grounds, who, stepping up to him, inquires if he remembers that the time is rapidly approaching for his annual celebration, and whether he thinks that Pat, the Hibernian, really means to put into execution the threats he has pronounced against him. Our boy replied that he did not apprehend any trouble at all, and that he saw no reason why he should not celebrate his particular holiday as well as any other sect or nationality, who are all allowed the privilege.

"As long," he continued, "as there is no rule against such demonstrations, your claim to avail yourself of the same rights as others cannot be disputed, although, I must say, for my own part, I would much rather see you all more American in feeling, and leave your foreign celebrations on the other side of the water."

"We are not really so much interested in celebrating the anniversary," replied the Orange boy, "were it not for the

Getting ready for the Twelfth.

brutal treatment we received last year, the threats that
have been constantly uttered against us since, and the principle of right and wrong that is involved.   Am I alone to
be singled out for exclusion from your republican liberty
and freedom for no fault of my own whatever?"

"Certainly not," said our boy; and here they parted,
and he thought no more of the subject.

As the time approached, however, for the Orange celebration, the air grew dark with threatening rumors.

Pat, the Hibernian, seemed to be working himself up to

a high pitch of excitement about the matter, even to tear-
ing off orange-colored ribbons from the persons of those entirely uninterested in his quarrels, although he saw fit to
flaunt his own " wearing of the green" before every eye,
whether offensive or not.   Whether he was egged on by his
Jesuitical advisers, to whom obedience was, with him, a duty
of much greater consequence than loyalty to Miss Columbia, or whether his fiery imagination was inflamed by the
exciting tunes that were played by his own special trumpet-

The Irish Blower.

ers, did not appear openly, but many conjectures were
started as to whether his opposition had a leader.

His feelings soon found expression in a meeting held by the

The Hibernian meeting.

Hibernians, who gave warning of the most bloodthirsty intentions if the Orange celebration was allowed to take place, and, moreover, of the withdrawal of their voice from the party which they had hitherto supported.

The Jesuits publicly desired their flocks to desist from violence if, as they said, "this insulting demonstration is persisted in," which must have appeared to Pat something like setting two dogs to fight each other, and then pulling one gently back by the tail.

Then, on the morning before the day of the celebration, the head boy of the Tammany section, Oakey Pokey, posted up a proclamation prohibiting the Orange procession.

" DON'T."

Bill Poster.

When the boys saw this posted around, their indignation was very great. Miss Columbia appeared to share this feeling with them, but controlled herself and said nothing, as it was from the boys themselves that a movement must come.

While these angry emotions were in full force, a proclamation was issued by the boy in charge of the adjoining section, giving the Orange boy full liberty to parade, and promising him protection to the fullest extent of his power. This decision our loyal boys applauded so loudly that the Tammany boys began to see that they had made a mistake, and to fear that the tide of public feeling was turning so strongly against them, that, in the contest approaching, their own dazzling careers would be brought to an untimely end.

They seem to have been used to considering this section

their own and Pat's for so long, to rule just as they liked, that they believed there was really no end to the endurance of the honest boys.

They had hitherto calculated on their own irresistible strength, with their fingers always pilfering the public treasury, and with the giant force of the Irish boy to back them. They did not think this last bold stroke of theirs would be the spark to light the long dormant fire of American patriotism.

American patience and toleration is long-suffering indeed, but a turning-point comes at last. This was not like fighting among brothers, as was the case in that great uprising ten years before. This was an Irish invasion, led by a few

The Invasion, led by American Traitors.

corrupt American traitors and demagogues. This was crushing the serpent, warmed at the hearthstone, who turns and stings its benefactor. This was the most bigoted member of one sect interfering with the rights of the State and setting its rules at defiance.

These sentiments were freely expressed all over the school, and the most intense indignation and contempt was manifested for the cowards who thought fit to surrender so basely to the mob, no matter how strong it might be. The leaders of the Tammany section were denounced in the strongest terms, even by those who had hitherto followed their lead blindly.

Startled.

Then, at the eleventh hour, the Tammany boys sent for Johnny T., one of their members, whose connection with them, they thought, threw a halo of respectability over the whole gang. He, innocent that he was, "was only that moment apprised of the actual state of affairs," and had never dreamed of such a thing as mischief brewing, especially among his own constituents !

He was enlightened, however, in words so urgent, that ho felt that further vacillation would not answer, so he rapidly betook himself to the threatened scene of violence, issued a counter-proclamation, when it was too late for more than a handful of Orange boys to assemble, allowing them

Halfman and Staff.

the right to parade, calling at the same time upon the
members of the police and militia to keep the peace, thus
making the fact plain enough that the Tammany leaders
themselves were trembling before their own chosen.

" Who's Boss?"

The pliant tools, whose ignorance and credulity they had
turned to such profitable account for so long, were at length
becoming too sharp for them.

All that night, active preparations went on among the police and the militia boys; they were determined that, let the morrow bring what it might, it should find them ready. Among them there was perfect unanimity. All seemed to feel that the time had now come to assert themselves, and end this degrading servility to a lawless mob and its dishonest leaders.

The eventful day came, and it was noticed that most of the Tammany boys made themselves very scarce, doubtless waiting for the whole thing to "blow over." Many of them left that section, deeming it best for their personal safety; and those that remained, with happy instinct, sought shelter at police headquarters.

The militia turned out at the appointed hour, and many of them, as they passed by the great commander-in-chief, Johnny T., inwardly cursed him in their hearts for the bloody work they now had to perform; for it was through him and his colleagues that the Irish mob had grown so strong and defiant; and now that their daring was about to assume a violent form, he coolly appealed to the militia and police for protection.

The handful of Orange boys who had been notified in time that the parade was to be allowed now formed, and the police and militia formed around them. The procession now began to move—they marched to the tune of the "Star-Spangled Banner." They did not even attempt to play the so-called insulting, air of "Croppies, lie down,"

which every Irish Catholic boy considers sufficient provoca-
tion for raising a row; but perhaps this national American
air was equally offensive and heretical, for, as it was, the
fast-increasing mob commenced the assault. Threatening
menaces were heard from them, some exclaiming, "Ah!
see the British soldiers!" as if that were the most stinging
taunt. Then a perfect storm of missiles assailed them, and
shots were fired from every direction. Some of our boys
fell, and then our brave militia returned the fire, and many
a Croppie lay down never to rise again.

"Croppies, lie down."

The mob began to see that the militia was really in
earnest, and that blank cartridges were not the order of
the day this time.

This startling revelation acted upon them like magic,
and the procession was allowed to go on its way with no
further disorder among the mob than the police themselves
were able to deal with, which they did with a courage and

THE LATE UNPLEASANTNESS. (Twelfth of July.)

bravery that made the whole school resound with their praise.

The procession reached its destination, and was quietly dismissed, and that section of the school never spent a more peaceful night than the one which gave place to this turbulent day.

Next morning, when the school was assembled, Miss Columbia expressed her approbation in the warmest terms of the prompt manner in which the Irish mob had been dealt with, and of the short time in which order had been restored, in spite of the usurpers' strength. Now the odium of public opinion began to fall with crushing weight upon the Tammany leaders. The Eleventh-Hour Johnny T., as

Between two fires.

he was now called, found himself between two fires ; he was condemned by both parties. The loyal boys were indignant at his dalliance with so great an evil, and his own supporters were enraged at his daring to try to preserve the peace against their will, and he caught it all round, as miserable pretenders generally do at last.

114 JULY

As to Oakey Pokey, he was lauded to the skies by the low mob, and the "Know-Nothing" of old times now became a great Irish patriot! What next? The Irish boys now held many indignation meetings, protesting against Johnny T. Halfman, calling him a Dutch butcher, and vowed that when they

Up like a rocket.

Down like the stick.

pledged themselves to give him their support, they were assured that everything obnoxious to them should be abolished, and that his recent conduct was a violation of his trust, and that he ought, consequently, to be swept out of his place and power.

At some of these meetings they proposed to form themselves into invincible organizations, so that they might carry all before them with irresistible force next time they saw fit to do so.

It became evident, however, that the time was hardly ripe yet for further demonstration, from the quietness of the Jesuits and from the subdued tunes which some of the Catholic trumpets now played.

" Left blooming alone."

Thus Croppie was left for awhile, in the midst of his wild talk, without any leadership; the Tammany boys were shy of him temporarily, and the Jesuit kept prudently in the background. The Tammany boys, although their bravado seemed to have no limit hitherto, had been shaking in their shoes ever since the riot; for, in addition to the disgrace which that brought upon them, one of the

The Times (not) out of joint.

boldest boys in the section had been exposing some of their secret accounts, which publicly revealed the enor-

mous frauds which they had perpetrated for some time
past, and showed the honest boys but too plainly where
layer after layer of the gigantic tacks had come from,
which had aggravated them so sorely, and of late had
grown unendurable. The rumors of the meetings and the
threats of vengeance pronounced there reached Miss Columbia, and one morning she thus addressed the school:

"Many of the boys have come to me since the outbreak
of the 12th of July, and besought me to use my influence
to prevent this thing from becoming a religious dispute.

" Got enough ?"

Now, I ask you, who is it that insists upon making it so? Who is it that says that, 'while the State has rights, she has them only in virtue and by permission of the superior authority, which can only be expressed through the Church?' Who is it that denies the right of any one to the ballot except in 'subordination to the Church?' Who is it that declares that the 'Catholic, armed with his vote, is the. champion of law, order, faith and morality?' Who is it that states that 'every Catholic is bound to acknowledge himself, as a voting citizen, a passive instrument in the hands of the Roman hierarchy, and is bound to use his suffrage power in such a way as may most speedily put the education of the whole people within the direct control of the hierarchy, since to falter in meeting this demand is disloyalty to God, because it is treason against the divine sovereignty of the Church?' Who is it that says, 'Let the public school go to the devil, where it came from?' Can we shut our eyes to the meaning of such sentiments? No! we dare not; we must rouse ourselves from our lethargy, we must meet our antagonist with his own weapons, and he must learn to keep his religion to himself, as the rest of us do. We must look this evil in the face, and not call it by any other name, or shirk it in any way. If they persist in crying, 'Down with black Protestantism!' we must also inscribe upon our banners, 'Anti-Irish-*Political*-Roman-Catholic-Party.'

"They give the weight of all their power as Catholics, and we must counteract it as anti-Catholics. Look back into history. What has been the result in every country where the Catholic Church has had complete sway ? Don't let us have a repetition of that here !

"We acknowledge that among liberal Catholics there are many worthy and estimable ones, who never dream of intruding their religion into state affairs, but who are able to consider matters of government without reference to Church. For such as those we have only feelings of fra-

Roused at last.

ternal fellowship, but for those turbulent bigots, who are continually dragging their Church into national affairs, there is no course left us but to compel them to conform to our rules, or to go back where they came from.   It is not *their* country, as they seem to think; it belongs equally to all of us.   All are welcome, irrespective of creed, color, or nationality, and all have equal rights.

"Now, boys," she continued, "argument will never con-

The uprising.

vince our would-be usurper; and all that talking can do,
with regard to our difficulties, has been done. We must
have no more beating about the bush; and the sooner he
understands his relation to us and to our school, the better.
One thing is certain, the longer he puts it off, the
worse it will be. Then, boys, I say, rally round the flag;
be fearless, just, and upright, and, above all, be united, and
you are sure of victory!"

And the air was rent with cheer upon cheer, and the en-
thusiasm was so prolonged and hearty, that Miss Columbia
felt assured that "the American idea would *never* have to
give way to the Catholic idea."

The result.

" RENDER UNTO CÆSAR THE THINGS THAT
ARE CÆSAR'S, AND TO GOD THE THINGS
THAT ARE GOD'S."—Mark 12 : 17.

Harper's Magazine.

The great design of *Harper's* is to give correct information and rational amusement to the great masses of the people. There are few intelligent American families in which *Harper's Magazine* would not be an appreciated and highly welcome guest. There is no monthly Magazine an intelligent reading family can less afford to be without. Many Magazines are accumulated. *Harper's* is edited. There is not a Magazine that is printed which shows more intelligent pains expended on its articles and mechanical execution. There is not a cheaper Magazine published. There is not, confessedly, a more popular Magazine in the world.—*New England Homestead.*

Harper's Weekly.

It has become a very powerful organ of political opinion. Its leading articles on domestic and foreign questions and political events are distinguished by weight of argument and force of style, while never offensive in tone nor transcending the limits of cultivated journalism. The plan on which it is conducted necessitates the reliance upon foreign sources for the illustration of events occurring in Europe and other parts of the Old World, although original sketches, sent from abroad, are frequently engraved for its pages; and some of the best pictures it has given have been from the pencils of American artists. Among these we may mention the powerful political cartoons of Mr. Nast, which, for several years, have been a prominent feature in the paper.—*N. Y. Times.*

Harper's Bazar.

Free from all political and sectarian discussion, devoted to fashion, pleasure, and instruction, it is just the agreeable, companionable, and interesting domestic paper which every mother and wife and sweet-heart will require every son, husband, and lover to bring home with him every Saturday evening.—*Philadelphia Ledger.*

TERMS FOR 1872.

HARPER'S MAGAZINE, One Year $4 00
HARPER'S WEEKLY, One Year 4 00
HARPER'S BAZAR, One Year 4 00
HARPER'S MAGAZINE, HARPER'S WEEKLY, and HARPER'S BAZAR, to one address, for one year, $10 00; or any two for $7 00.

An Extra copy of either the MAGAZINE, WEEKLY, *or* BAZAR *will be supplied gratis for every* FIVE SUBSCRIBERS *at* $4 00 *each, in one remittance; or Six Copies for* $20 00, *without extra copy.*

www.ingramcontent.com/pod-product-compliance
Lightning Source LLC
Chambersburg PA
CBHW031454270326
41930CB00007B/998